BARREN
BUT
NOT BROKEN

A Journey from Infertility to Adoption

Foreword/Introduction

I am such a lover of literature and reading. I cannot remember a time in my life that I didn't just want to pick up a book, go to a place where I could be alone and read until the book was finished. Since I was a child, I would read a book in a very particular manner. First, I would read the front inner cover that gave a description of the book. Then I would jump to the back cover with the book reviews. Finally, I would head over to the inner back spine that taught me more about the author, review the index and right before diving into the book I would read the foreword aka the intro. I think I did this because I was so anxious to learn exactly what the book I was reading is about. What I discovered from the manner in which I read a book was that there is nothing more annoying than an extremely long introduction, which the author hides as their true first chapter. So, with that in mind, I will keep it short, sweet and to the point…

Sir Frances Galton theorized that we are who we are based on nature and nurture. Since 1869 people have debated what force shapes who we are? Some say that we are who we are based on our genetic makeup – this is nature. I have always wondered whether my strong desire to be a mother was based on how I was raised, by a very strong and nurturing mother, or whether it is a natural consequence of my genetic makeup. Either way, I've always had a very strong desire to be a mom. Thus, this book and the story of my journey to motherhood.

I must put a few disclaimers out in the atmosphere before you proceed. What did you expect – I'm an attorney! First and foremost, I have a Juris Doctorate in Law, but I am not a medical doctor. In this book I will use a lot of medical terminology. Second, I do not represent that I am a physician with the ability to diagnose any type of medical condition. When I discuss medical terms, I am using the information I acquired during my journey with infertility.

This book was written with certain people in mind. It is written for every woman who has dreamed or is dreaming of becoming a mother but had her dream derailed or denied. It is written for every man hat desired or who still desires to see a little image of himself in the world one day. I write this to every person, couple, straight, gay, transgender, White, Black, Asian, Latino, old, young, liberal, conservative, and of various religious backgrounds and socioeconomic standings who one day dream of being called mommy or daddy.

There are several reasons why you have chosen to read this book. One of the obvious reasons is that you desire to become a parent again or for the first time. It is also quite possible that you are reading this book to better understand what infertility and family creation looks like through the lenses of an infertile person. For whatever reason you have chosen to read this book, I hope that my story can help you on your journey to parenthood and/or understanding infertility.

Once you have finished reading this book, I hope that you are enlightened and encouraged after hearing my story. For years I struggled with telling my story to anyone because I thought no one cared about what I have gone through on my journey of becoming a parent. It wasn't until very recently that I discovered that there are a multitude of people who desire to know more about family creation, infertility and adoption and that by not sharing my testimony I was doing all those people a disservice. I would meet random strangers, on a flight or at a party, who would open up and tell me of their desire to become a parent. Listening to these people really motivated me to tell the story. Now is the time! So, put on your seatbelt and enjoy the ride.

In sharing my story, the first thing I had to overcome is that little voice inside my head that kept telling me I had a story no one wanted to hear. Or the second little voice that said, "you are not famous, so why would anyone listen"? I began to believe the little voice more than my own self and I began to ask myself, "why would anyone read my story"? No, I am not famous! Although on some days I feel like the Queen of England, Beyoncé, Sojourner Truth and Bono morphed into one amazing human being. On those days, you can't tell me I am not as big of a deal as Oprah! Even though I am not famous, I am so much more like you, the very real person who is reading this book at this very moment. I am the optimistic person that dreamed of doing something that so many other humans had done before me…REPRODUCE.

I have gone through so many things in my journey to become a mom that has caused me much strife. Yet, these same struggles have brought about development, growth, deliverance, and wisdom. I am not defined by the tragedy that I have gone through to become a parent. So many chains have been broken by my decision to reveal my story. Some of the things that I have been allowed to go through, even chosen to go through has brought me right to this current place in time where my words may help you. Some of what I must share, I don't want to, but in obedience to God I feel I need to share my whole truth. Doesn't the truth set you free…enter the journey to my freedom.

Special thanks to Michael Pierson for your support in this process, I love you. I dedicate this book to Justice and Aiden because it's the story of how we found each other. Mommy loves you both!

CHAPTER ONE

Three Hundred and Sixty-Five Plus One

PREGNANCY 1: THE ABORTION, THE STORY I DIDN'T WANT TO TELL, BUT THAT I MUST TELL!

My entire life I have worked diligently to acquire the things that I wanted. Call it luck or favor, many of the things that I worked for came easily to me. I excelled academically and was involved in several activities. By the time I was 9 years of age, I was deemed a gift and talented child by the administrators and educators at the elementary school I was attending. I was placed in the G.A.T.E. (gifted and talented education) Program. Each year I received every academic award the school offered. At age 13, I was the only female advancing to computer coding competitions around the country. By the end of junior high I was taking college courses. I accomplished so much academically, yet I never felt beautiful. I struggled with my self-confidence and felt like boys probably did not find me attractive.

The summer before my freshman year of high school I met a young man by the name of Teir. A mutual friend introduced us on a hot summer day. We took one look into each other's eyes and had no chemistry. Both Teir and I did not find one another attractive. Teir, whose name means drought, was very interesting but not my type.

He didn't have a dry personality, he just didn't look like the type of guy I usually found attractive. What was my type? Pretty boys! I usually spooned over the guys that were so pretty that they spent more time in the bathroom grooming than I did. Teir on the other hand was an athlete. He threw on a sweatshirt, tee shirt and pair of jeans each day and didn't spend much time coordinating his attire. He was a very funny and easy-going guy. We began to speak on the phone, and he began to teach me not to sweat the small stuff nor worry about those things that seemed so giant in the moment. Teir and I became best friends and our friendship grew into a budding relationship.

I wasn't a fast girl, not promiscuous like many of the girls I went to school with. I didn't want to be what people thought an Oakland, California Stereotypical teenage girl from a single-family household was. In the late 80's and early 90's that stereotype was that a girl like me, being raised in a low income, single parent household was a promiscuous girl, possibly a teenage mom on government assistance. I refused to be boy crazed and promiscuous. I focused on my school work and church. I stayed in church, joined various educational groups and clubs, and was often referred to as "

"Miss Goody Two Shoes". Despite my vow to be different, Teir and I began having sexual intercourse when I was 15½ years of age. We were so young and had not really discussed the possibility of me becoming pregnant. My mom had no idea I was sexually active, nor did she know I had a boyfriend. During those years I wasn't allowed to speak to a boy on the phone. The only interaction I was supposed to have with the opposite sex was at school or with my male family members. I was raised in the church, sang with my mother and grandmother in the church choir and wasn't allowed to go to school games or other extra-curricular events without taking my younger cousins. My grandmother and I shared a bedroom and spent a lot of time around one another. I was not able to speak on the phone with Teir and thus I snuck around to date Teir.

By my Junior year I discovered that my school was going to skip me past a grade and that I would not have to complete senior year in high school. I was completing high school in three years and preparing my college applications to U.C. Berkeley, Tuskegee University, and Spelman College. My high school threw a dance called "The Winter Ball". I really wanted to go with Teir. However, my mother still had no idea that I had a boyfriend. In order to go to he dance, I had to finally revealed to my mom that I had a boyfriend. My mother allowed Teir to pick me up. She took a copy of his driver's license. As Teir and I began to exit my house to proceed to the Winter Ball my mother informed us that we had to take my younger cousins with us on a date. After that date Teir was allowed to come over more often.

Teir graduated high school in 1995 and went straight to Morehouse College in Atlanta Georgia. The following year I graduated high school and was admitted to Tuskegee University in Alabama. Both Colleges are historical black colleges and Teir and I would only be two hours from one another. The summer before my freshman year, I learned Teir and I were pregnant. As soon as I discovered I was pregnant, I called Teir and told him. His reaction was not what I expected. For the first time in our relationship Teir, normally a cool cucumber, sounded worried. He told me that he couldn't have a child at this point in his life and that he didn't want to let his parents down. After our conversation, I had a hard time reaching Teir by phone as he would no longer take my calls or answer my pages to his pager. Yes, I said pager, as cellular phones were on the horizon and not so common in the early 90's. I felt so alone and didn't know what to do.

I decided to tell my mom to seek her advice. I never really wanted to go tell this news to my mom because I was afraid of letting her down and making her upset. My mother raised me by herself and at that time in my life I did everything to make her happy. I will never forget the moment that I told her I was pregnant. I was sitting in my room with the television on. I slowly began telling my mother the most devastating news I had to offer at that point in my little seventeen years on the planet. After telling my mother, she got quiet and thought before she spoke. She looked up at the television that was on and said "you see that lady laying on the beach on TV? That's how I see you having everything, being wealthy, and doing great things. A baby is a blessing but will slow all of that down." As I began to cry, my mother said, "I am here for you for whatever you choose but I really want you to go to college". My mother and my grandmother asked me to stay home for college and raise my baby. I was so afraid and confused. I knew I did not want to be a single mom. A week later, I had my mother schedule an abortion with Kaiser Hospital.

On the morning I was scheduled to have an abortion, I still had not heard from Teir. My mother drove me to the hospital. My mother and I listen to the medical staff tell us the details of the procedure. They never really acknowledged me and spoke directly to my mother. The staff informed my mother that the procedure would take a little over 2 hours and immediately thereafter I would go into the recovery room. After my mother left, the medical staff inserted an IV bag and I met with an anesthesiologist who informed me that I would go to sleep and wake up after the procedure, pregnant no more. As they wheeled me down to the treatment room, I yelled, "Hey, I change my mind, I want my baby". I told them to stop, but no one listened to me and told me it was the medication speaking, that my mother had already left and that they had to proceed. I remember feeling like I was in the twilight zone, because no one was listening to me. The doctors were talking about what they ate for lunch and about their own children to one another. I felt invisible in one of the scariest and sacred moments of my life.

Before going into the procedure, I can describe the feeling of pregnancy like feeling full as one feels after eating a large meal. However, after the procedure I felt empty. I asked the staff for my mother, but she wasn't there. I later discovered that she had gone to the movies while I was being treated because she thought the procedure was going to take two hours. The medical staff had me get up and put on my clothing and leave the facility. I stood outside alone. My mother saw me and became upset that they gave her the wrong information as to the amount of time the procedure would take and that they just had me leave the facility. After the procedure, instead of going home, my mother took me to lunch with my aunts and cousins. I just wanted to go home and be alone in my thoughts, but instead I felt like it was a bit of a celebration of my loss. On that same day, Teir finally called to talk about what we should do about the baby, but it was too little too late. I would harbor anger towards him for years after the decision. I harbored even more anger towards myself for my decision to get an abortion. I eventually forgave myself and Teir, but my forgiveness did not manifest for nearly 20 years later.

I have had so much shame in my decision to abort my baby and even contemplated not writing about it in this book. Many of us punish ourselves for the decisions that we've made, decisions that we can no longer take back. I allowed myself to live in shame for so many years as I punished myself for aborting my pregnancy. Years after I foolishly concluded that I was not getting pregnant as a punishment from God for the abortion. Hindsight is 20/20, because now I know that God had long forgiven me and that I needed to forgive myself. Once I released myself from the guilt, shame and punishment, it was as if I had lifted a weight off my shoulders.

Dearest one reading this book. If you have ever decided that you are not proud of, please remember to give yourself grace. You cannot bring that moment back, yet you can press forward. It is time to forgive yourself so that you can free yourself from the bondage that you have probably been holding yourself captive. It is not until you accept that you decided based on what you felt you had to do at the time and forgive your disappointments, that you can move closer to your destiny.

PREGNANCY 2: THE MISCARRIAGE

After the abortion Teir and I broke up. I took off for Tuskegee University and isolated myself during that first year of college. I was suffering from depression, shame and guilt. I had trust issues and decided that I didn't want to get close to many people, out of fear of getting hurt. Eventually Teir and I talked and dated on and off throughout college. Teir finished college in 1999. During that summer, before my senior year in college and we became pregnant again. After learning that we were pregnant we began working with a realtor to purchase a home. I was 21 and Teir was 22 years of age, but we were very ready to step up to our responsibility. After an initial reaction of fear, we began to get excited about a little person entering our life. When I passed my first trimester, I began working with my step father as a summer intern at a Toyota Logistics Facility in Fremont, California. One day after work, I began to feel cramping and pain. Teir and my mom took me to the hospital to be checked out. The doctor rolled in an ultrasound machine and began to look at the baby and listen for the baby's heartbeat. In my gut I knew something was wrong with the baby and could not pull myself to look at the monitor. Teir looked and to this day tells me that he saw our child. The doctor told me that the baby was extremely underdeveloped for me to be so far along. He further stated that I was losing the baby and that the child would not make it to term due to a failure to thrive. I was informed that the pregnancy would result in a miscarriage shortly. I was given medicine to induce labor and within a week I began to miscarry. We lost the baby five months into the pregnancy. Our loss was devastating.

Teir and I tried to cope with this loss, but we decided to go our separate ways. Even though God had forgiven me for my abortion, I had yet to forgive myself. I constantly told myself that my baby died because I had killed his sibling by aborting my pregnancy when I was 17. I didn't know that I was suffering from depression and tried to keep myself busy to deal with it. I decided to go to graduate school to work on my Ph.D. in Organizational Development. Teir buried himself in his work at his new job.

A miscarriage can have a damaging effect on any relationship and on a person's mental wellbeing. For some reason, since my baby was never born, I felt as if it had never existed and that my pregnancy wasn't equivalent to the successful pregnancies of others. People tried to console me with comments such as "you will eventually have a baby", "God loved your baby too much to let it see this world", "you want one of my kids?", "at least you didn't meet the baby that would have been harder than losing it once you've seen it". All these statements people made to console a parent grieving their unborn child can be received as ignorant, insensitive and offensive. They do nothing but make healing a little more difficult. I understand it's hard to find the right words to say to someone when they've lost a loved one that has actually been born. So, having the right words for the loss of the unborn can be even more difficult. Sometimes the best response to a person who has just miscarried is no response. A listening ear and a moment of silent reflection can go a long way.

DAY 1 TO DAY 365

Years later Teir and I found our way back to one another. We had moved from California to the District of Columbia. We lived in a small condo, only 600 square feet. Teir moved to D.C. on 9-11. I moved in a year later. I had been in D.C. for only one week when one day as I was unpacking my bags, Teir came into the bedroom and asked me to marry him. It was the worst proposal ever. He told me that he had a plan to take me to beautiful Union Station to propose marriage. He claimed that my bad proposal was my fault because as I unpacked, I kept going near his ring hiding spot. What can I say, the man did not have a romantic bone in his body.

After he proposed we decided not to have sex an entire year before our wedding. We did it, but it was hard (no pun intended)! We were in love, on our way to getting married, alone for the first time in our lives, in a hot city, in a very small condo. It took lots of cold showers and sleeping in separate spaces to get through. Washington D.C. was such a fun place for a young childless couple. We rode our bikes around the nation's capital, to the Cherry Blossom Festival and concerts at the national mall. The fun ended once the coldest winter I had ever experienced rolled in. The D.C. Sniper Shootings began, and I begged Teir to go back home. In July of 2003, we rented our condo out and purchased a condominium in Hayward, California.

We were married on August 31, 2003 in front of 300 guests. Go figure we were so tired after our overly large wedding that we fell asleep before we could have sex. However, the day after the wedding we were so excited to have sex and even more to have baby making sex. I just knew I would get pregnant just by him looking at me. Why wouldn't I? My grandmother had nine children and my great grandmother had nine children. Plus, I ignorantly thought "black women don't problems having children".

Every month my period came, I thought that it was just God giving us more time to spend childless to strengthen our union. However, I would tell myself that my positive pregnancy test was on the horizon in the coming months. Before I knew it we were planning our one-year anniversary and I still was not pregnant. At the brink of our one-year anniversary I was completing my first year of law school (getting married, starting law school and trying to have a baby at one time is a whole other story, but let's just say I am an overachiever). I figured that I had not gotten pregnant due to the stress of law school. I talked to Teir about going to see a gynecologist to see if there was anything, we could do to maximize our chances of getting pregnant. We went to see an OB/GYN in Hayward, California. She did an examination and asked us lots of questions. After the exam the doctor asked Teir and I to join her in her office. In that office my biggest fears were actualized. The doctor told me that after one year, three hundred and sixty-five days, of trying to get pregnant there was a likelihood that there were some issues with fertility that prohibited our ability to become pregnant. It was like a ton of bricks had landed on my dreams and buried them away in that moment. I could not understand anything the doctor said after that because her words began to sound like Charlie Brown's Teacher "wah wah wah wah wah". Since we were at 365 plus days of trying to get pregnant, she made a referral to Stanford Hospital Gynecology to determine whether we had any fertility issues.

Teir and I were both very quiet on the ride home. He tried to make me feel better by saying "Babe maybe it's me". I intuitively knew that I was the "problem" and not him. I think I always had a feeling that as badly as I wanted to be a mom, I would have issues conceiving. To this day I still cannot verbalize why I felt this way. In our true Teir and Patanisha Fashion we decided to take a staycation to Monterey and Carmel to try not to think about the news we had just received. However, if we would have been completely honest it was the only thing on our minds during the entire trip.

CHAPTER TWO

INFERTILITY? REALLY?

DAY 366

The World Health Organization (WHO) defines infertility as a disease of the reproductive system defined by the failure to achieve a clinical pregnancy after 12 months or more of regular unprotected sexual intercourse. Here I was 25 years old asking myself "Am I infertile?". Forewarning, this chapter discusses lots of medical terminology. Remember, I'm not a medical doctor. I just lived this. Growing up I heard the stories of the women who didn't have babies. Some of them involved the woman who couldn't find a husband, the woman whose husband couldn't have babies, the woman hat drank turpentine because she just didn't want a baby, the woman that only cared about her career and didn't have time for a baby. I kept hearing different versions of this woman who had no children. Once we hit 364 days plus one of marriage, people began to talk openly about me as if I was the woman from these stories. At the law school I attended, an African American Woman who was supposed to be there to encourage and mentor newly admitted students pulled me aside and told me that I needed to make a choice to either have children or become a lawyer. A relative of my husband told me that it was selfish of me to focus on my career and that if I just ate some double yoked eggs, I could get pregnant (go figure it could be that easy). A stranger that I had met in a social setting told me that if I just stopped taking birth control, which I wasn't on, my husband and I could start our family. People began to think it was ok to talk to me about something so personal like my womb, sex with my husband, medications they assumed I was taking, and my family planning. In hindsight, I should have spoken up to each and every inappropriate person. I was such a people pleaser I did not have the courage to speak up. Please remember to protect your feelings and decide with your partner just how much you would like to share. Never feel obligated to share in an attempt to be kind. Family creation is a private topic that no one should think they are entitled to receive information or give unsolicited advice. What none of the naysayers knew was that I wanted to be nothing like the woman described at the beginning of this chapter. I desired so deeply in my heart to be a mom. At that time the only way that I knew how to become a mom was by getting pregnant which I had yet accomplished. I decided to make an appointment at Stanford to speak with the OB/GYN regarding my inability to get pregnant within the first year of my marriage. I went to my appointment at

Stanford and meet an amazing doctor. She listened to Teir and I describe the frequency of our lovemaking, among other things. She decided that she would test our egg and sperm quality and count. Teir was asked to provide a sperm sample. They informed him that he could do a sample at Stanford or bring one in. After two long minutes in a private room, Teir provided them with a sample.

I took the Clomid Challenge Test to determine by blood the number of eggs reserved in my ovaries. This test began for me on day one of my cycle. I came to the office and had my blood drawn to determine my Estradiol and Follicle Stimulating Hormone levels. The test looked at the ovaries ability to produce eggs. Days after the first blood test I had to take a pill called Clomid (Clomiphene Citrate) and then days later repeated the same blood test taken on day one. I was informed that one of the side effects of taking Clomid was the possibility of multiples (babies) if I became pregnant during that menstrual cycle. My blood results showed, drum roll please....

Great news! I had a good quality of eggs and Teir had great swimmers. Teir and I could not understand why we weren't getting pregnant? I had always been a sill optimist my entire life. I secretly believed that I would get pregnant with twins right after doing the Clomid Challenge Test. This never happened and I scheduled my return appointment to the doctor to determine my next diagnostic test. The next step was to go back to the doctor to discuss my next steps. After a very long examination and discussion my doctor began to explain a condition called "Endometriosis". Endometriosis is a disorder in which tissue that normally grows within the endometrium (the lining inside the uterus), begins to grow outside of the uterus. This tissue has no clue its planting in the wrong place and acts as normal by thickening and bleeding each period. Endometriosis causes scar tissue and adhesion to organs. This disorder affects fertility. The doctor informed me that I may have developed Endometriosis and that she needed to do a surgical procedure to determine what fertility problems I suffer from. I had a two-part procedure: laparoscopy and hysterosalpingography. The hysterosalpingography is an x-ray of the uterus and fallopian tubes and is done vaginally. The radiologist pushes dye through the tubes and uterus while capturing the picture through x-ray. At the same time that I was having this done the surgeon performed the laparoscopy which involved her making a two to three-inch horizontal incision at the bikini line. Once she made the incision, she placed a laparoscope in through the opening to look at my female reproductive organs. Immediately after the surgery I learned that I had a little endometriosis, but my main issue was my fallopian tubes. Below is a picture of a woman's reproductive system.

FEMALE REPRODUCTIVE SYSTEM

Once a woman ovulates an egg comes from her ovary and is pulled into the fallopian tube. Fertilization, the sperm meeting the egg, usually occurs in the fallopian tube. The fertilized egg, also known as the embryo, makes its journey to the uterus where it implants in the lining, develops into a fetus and is born 9 months later.

A healthy fallopian tube has fimbriae at the end of it and is clear from blockage. Fimbria are like little fingers at the top of the fallopian tubes closest to the ovary. The fimbria helps pull the egg into the tube after ovulation. In my case, I have clubbed fimbriae on one tube and the other tube was blocked. The doctor found that with the issues with my tubes it would be best for us to try to conceive through In-Vitro Fertilization (IVF).

I had never heard of IVF, nonetheless, a black person ever doing it. I heard a comedian, Robin Harris (now deceased), making jokes about test tube babies, but nothing beyond that. So, what was IVF? We had no clue about the journey we were about to embark upon, but we were excited about the possibility of being one step closer to being parents.

CHAPTER THREE

IVF

At 26 years of age I was confronted with the reality that if I wanted to give birth to a baby, I would have to do In Vitro Fertilization (IVF). I had no clue what IVF entailed or how much it would cost. All I knew was that I was determined to do whatever it took to become pregnant and become a mom. After my laparoscopy and hysterosalpingogram my gynecologist referred me to Stanford Hospital Infertility Clinic. There I met a wonderful team of fertility doctors. During my first appointment I met with the physician who reviewed my medical records.

Teir and I both attended the appointment. The doctor informed us that IVF involved retrieval of unfertilized eggs from me, sperm from Teir and the process of fertilization outside of the body. Once fertilization occurred the physician would then transfer the embryo into my uterus and await implantation. Sounded easy enough to me! The doctor was very optimistic that I would have no trouble getting pregnant due to my age and the number of eggs that I produced during the clomid challenge.

Once the doctor left the room, then we met with a financial representative. She informed me that the typical cost during that time for an IVF Procedure was approximately $10,000 to $15,000. She informed me that the medication was an additional cost and that it may cost up to an additional $5,000. WHAT!!!!! I naively responded, "but we have insurance". The lady slightly smiled and informed me that most insurance plans do not cover IVF. The lady informed me that Teir and I may qualify to be in a study that would cover the cost of our medication. Based on our age and ethnicity there was a Preimplantation Genetic Diagnosis, PGD Study. Teir and I would need to do some genetic testing, meet with the geneticist and be followed during our IVF Cycle.

We received a significant amount of information and decided to take a trip to Monterey, California to clear our heads and to decide whether or not we would do IVF. Take note that Teir and I developed a trend of traveling whenever we encountered stress or tough times. This was the first of many tough time trips. We were just a few months past our first year of marriage and we decided to celebrate with horseback rides on the beach and rides along the coastline. When we returned home, we decided to do IVF and the PGD Study.

The next question was how we would pay for the cycle. Teir contacted our medical insurance provider to determine if they would cover any of the cost of the IVF Cycle. They informed us that they would not cover any of the cost of the procedure, with exception to a few of the labs. However, none of the fertility medications were covered. Teir pulled money from his retirement, I asked our parents and my grandmother for loans and donations. I also did research to see if there were any grants or loans for fertility treatments, there were none. We did learn there was one manner in which we could get financial assistance in paying for our medication. Become guinea pigs by placing ourselves into a PGD Study!

THE PGD STUDY

Teir and I had no clue what a Preimplantation Genetic Diagnosis Study was. We were so naïve when it came to our general understanding of reproductive endocrinology. We were just happy that there was a program we qualified for that could provide us with discounted medication. We completed all the consents and terms of the study. The first stage of the PGD Study was to meet with the geneticist who asked us multiple questions about our family medical and socioeconomic history. This kind of felt like a counseling session. As it very long and dreadful hearing about family illnesses and predisposed genetic traits. Some of the questions included family medical history of cancer, questions about the health of our immediate family members, and how many children our family members have. The geneticist explained that PGD involved our going through the normal IVF cycle and once we have embryos, cells will be removed from the embryos to determine the health of the embryo. The healthy embryos will be placed into the uterus.

After we left the geneticist we were then sent to meet with the endocrinologist. She and the geneticist had arranged for us to do labs for the study and the IVF Cycle we were embarking on. After the lab work was completed, we returned to our room to meet with the physician and go over our IVF Schedule. The schedule I received was for a timespan of approximately one and a half months. It provided so much detail and outlined the entire process from start to the pregnancy test. When I got my IVF Schedule I felt like I had gotten the golden ticket from the Wonka Factory. I have attached a copy of my schedule on the next page.

REPRODUCTIVE ENDOCRINOLOGY
IVF CYCLE PATIENT OUTI **JENKINS,PATANISHA**   V# 1169217
ANTAGON/CETROTIDE PRO1 21314 GARY DRIVE #307
HAYWARD,CA 94545

DAY/DATE   F   HM# 510-888-9654

Now	Begin prenatal vitamins – as directed F60 1: 772 UNITED HEALTHCARE POS
‡ 4/24/05	Menses prior to oral contraceptive start.. CALL COORDINATOR (650) 498- *began on* 7911/Option #2 WITH THIS MENSES. Scheduled dates and appointments *04/26/05* generally stay the same even if menses is a few days later or earlier than projected.
‡ 4/29/05	ORAL CONTRACEPTIVE START DATE. Begin day 3 of menses. (Take active pills only. DO NOT take placebo pills). Continue through 5/24/05 ____(Stop pills as directed even if there is still something left in the packet. Call with questions.)
—	Hysteroscopy - (See hysteroscopy instructions.)Please check in 1 hour before appointment.
Thurs 5/19/05	7:15 a.m. – 10:00 a.m. Group IVF consult and injection training/review. ***NOTE***Bring 2 oranges, your partner and consent forms.
@ 930 Wed 5/25/05	BASELINE ULTRASOUND. BEGIN LOW DOSE ASPIRIN 81 mg one daily.If the consents and virology are not signed and submitted by this time, **WE WILL CANCEL THE CYCLE.**
Thurs 5/26/05	LAST DAY TO TAKE ORAL CONTRACEPTIVE.
‡ Sun 5/29/05	MENSES WILL OCCUR AFTER STOPPING OC. (Call only if menses does not start. Do not stop injecting meds if no menses until you discuss with coordinator.)
Tues 5/31/05	Begin Gonal-F ― IU / Follistim _225_ IU/ Repronex _75_ IU — Add when you start Total daily _300_ IU. *antagon* (Called 'cycle day 3' regardless of when your menses began.)
Fri 6/3/05	CYCLE DAY 6. Last day for vigorous exercise.
@ 970 Sat 6/4/05	CYCLE DAY 7. Ultrasound and possible estradiol blood test.
‡ mon 6/6/05	CYCLE DAY 9/10. Ultrasound and possible estradiol blood test. These will continue from now until hCG injection. DO NOT STOP GONAL-F, FOLLISTIM, REPRONEX until told to do so. LAST DAY FOR INTERCOURSE.
TBD	Begin daily morning injections of ANTAGON/CETROTIDE when told by MD - Continue daily until hCG injection.

••
SCHEDULE BELOW MAY VARY FROM 1-3 DAYS

‡ Sat 6/11/05	CYCLE DAY 14 most common day for EGG RETRIEVAL. Daily progesterone begins day after retrieval.
‡ Tues 6/14/05	may 3 Biopsy
‡ Thurs 6/16/05	CYCLE DAY 17/(9) most common day for day 3/(5) EMBRYO TRANSFER.
‥‥‥‥‥	PREGNANCY TESTS (hCG blood test) drawn in the REI Lab 13 days following egg retrieval. Have blood drawn between 8-10 a.m. for same day results.
‥‥‥‥‥	ULTRASOUNDS to confirm intrauterine pregnancy 4 and 6 weeks following embryo transfer.

IVF_Antagon_Cetrotide w/ pill
01-31-05 by: CSantos

Getting the schedule was exciting, but I felt like a little child getting her first library book or Dollie when the nurse handed me a bag of fertility medication and needles. I think in that moment, I was just excited to know that the contents of that bag would bring me one step closer to meeting our child. Now normally the nurses don't just come in with all your prescriptions in a bag and gift them to you. You usually get a prescription, call specialty pharmacies, spend thousands of dollars and order them. However, Teir and I were a part of the PGD Study, so we got a few of our injectable medications for free. Teir and I were never really told what was being studied nor if we were in the control or test group.

TO SHARE OR NOT TO SHARE? THAT IS THE QUESTION!

Once you and your significant other make a family plan, the next step is to decide whether you want to share your plan with others. In my situation, we had to decide whether to tell people or not? Teir is from a smaller family than my own. At his family events there are usually 10 to 15 people and most of them were his mother's friends. He is also much more private than I am. My family is huge! I am my mother's only child, but my mother is one of nine children.

When we have family events there are 50 to 75 people present. My family shares lots in our inner circle.

After a very lengthy discussion, Teir felt that we were the only two people that needed to know what we were doing. I on the other hand wanted to tell my mom, my grandmother, my best friend, my aunts, my cousins, the dog, and anyone else who would listen. I was so excited! We started off by just telling our mothers and my grandmother. If you know anything about a big family, news spreads like a wildfire. However, not many people knew what we were doing. They didn't find out until I ended up in the hospital with a medical emergency (I will tell you more about this later in the book). It was at that time that other family members shared and so did I. I told my best friend, cousin, and aunts what I was going through because I needed to lean on the women closest to me for mental support.

After sharing I found that people will always give you their opinion. They will either be very supportive, negative, worried, loving, or judgmental. You must remember that once you tell, you have opened the door to their feeling entitled to make comments. One of the most common things that people did was tell me about someone that they knew that got pregnant when she stopped trying. They made it sound so easy. They'd say "Pana (my nickname) if you guys would just stop thinking about it, relax, and stop trying you will get pregnant". However, when someone who has conceived easily simplifies your experience or medical condition it's a little offensive to say the least. The other comments that I heard was that IVF was like playing God. Someone literally said that If you didn't get pregnant on your own then maybe God didn't want me to be a parent. That's ignorant for lack of a better word. That's like saying you're playing God to get any help from a medical professional on a medical issue. People who knew I had an abortion asked me if I thought I was going through all this as a punishment from God. I was allowing people to resurrect the guilty thing that I know I had long been forgiven. As discussed earlier, I had to protect my own feelings and let people know when their comments became offensive.

Throughout your journey to become a parent the question, to tell or not to tell, will come up several times. You will also need to consider what it is you want to share. You will need to decide some of the following:

1. Do we tell that we are suffering from fertility issues?

2. Do we tell about our seeing a fertility doctor or taking tests?

3. Do we share our family building plan – IVF, IUI, Surrogacy, Adoption or to remain parentless?

4. Do we share our pregnancy?

5. Do we share our disappointments – miscarriage, selective reduction, failed IVF/IUI attempts?

6. Do we share the cost?

7. Do we share a successful adoption connection?

There is no right or wrong answer as to when and what to share. Sharing is a very personal decision. Now that I have lived this experience, I highly recommend sitting down with your partner to determine how much you both want to share and together find a happy compromise. I also recommend limiting the number of people that you tell. Fertility treatments are very interesting to those who lack full understanding and thus people tend to ask a lot of questions. The other benefit to limiting the number of people that you tell is that if your cycle does not result in a pregnancy that's less people that you have to tell that you are not pregnant. Find a safe community of people that you and your partner can vent to about your IVF Cycle. It may also be wise to educate your community on what an IVF Cycle entails and what type of support you both will need during the cycle. We discovered that many of the fertility clinics and adoption agencies have classes for family members. Check and see what resources are available on the web, in print, or at a facility for your family members to attend.

SHOULD YOU INJECT YOURSELF OR ALLOW SOMEONE ELSE TO INJECT YOU?

Most of the medication that one must take during the cycle is to be administered intravenously. When you receive your IVF Schedule, you will be trained on how to inject yourself or how someone should inject you. For more than two weeks, you can do two to three injections per day. Some of the medication is prefilled, while other must be drawn into a syringe to be administered. I was informed that I could inject myself in my stomach, buttocks, or in the thigh. I can take pain, but like most people I hate getting shots.

I was a little nervous by the thought of Teir injecting me. I think he was petrified by the thought of doing it himself. Let's just say that Teir has very large gross motor movements and he is not the gentlest of men. He means well, but I was afraid that he would break the needle in my skin when injecting, so I decided to be brave and inject myself.

The first time I had to administer a shot, I decided that I didn't want an audience and wanted to get through it alone. I didn't tell Teir what I was about to do. I just grabbed my medication and went into our small bathroom. I grabbed a handful of belly fat, took a deep breath and gave myself the shot. It was the first time I was so glad to have belly fat to grab on to.

I did it, but immediately thereafter I cried really hard. I cried because I felt sorry for myself that I had to go through this to get pregnant. I cried for the people who must give themselves shots daily based on a medical condition that requires regular doses of medication. My tears quickly turned to anger. I felt that it was so unfair that I had to do this when so many women took their pregnancies and their ability to get pregnant naturally for granted. I couldn't believe that just poking myself would spark so much emotion and I began to encourage myself with the thought that each time I poked myself I was one step closer to meeting my child.

A few years ago, I watched a reality television show that starred Evelyn Lozada, reality television star, business woman, author and mom. On the episode, Evelyn, who was undergoing IVF Treatments had to inject herself with medication. I can't express enough how emotional that show made me feel. I had so much empathy, compassion and connection for and to her experience.

When deciding how you want to receive your injections consider the following:

1. What time of day will you be injecting and whether you will have others around during that time of day to inject you? I always did my injections at a time that I knew no one would be present. I didn't want anyone to fawn over me or stare at me like I was a circus attraction. However, I've seen some women have friends come over, do it with their significant other holding their hand, or discreetly in a room full of people. There is no right or wrong choice.

2. Can you handle someone injecting you in the spaces that we consider private parts – buttocks,

love handles, thighs or your gut.

3. Think outside of the box. Most of us want our partner to help inject us, but this may be a task they may not be able to handle. Maybe you can seek assistance from a close friend, sibling, parent, or even a close co-worker. Make sure that this person is someone that you and your partner are comfortable with touching your body. Also, be mindful that once you invite someone in to help you, they will sometimes take it as though they now have the right to ask you very personal questions about your journey. Note: You should only share what you want and nothing more than that. As spoken of above, Evelyn Lozada invited people over for moral support when she did her injections, which is a very great idea.

4. Can you inject yourself? Heck yeah! It's a piece of cake. Hey, you're about to be a parent, you will do far more difficult and disgusting things. Like, clean a bunch of snot, wipe a nasty butt,

deal with excessive amounts of puke, and the list goes on. All you do is just grab the fat on your belly and 1,2,3, poke. Once you've done it the first time it's second nature.

SELECTIVE REDUCTION

At the onset of the IVF Cycle we were charged with deciding the number of embryos we would like transferred into my uterus. My initial response was "all of them". However, that response changed when they hit me with the second question. The second question was if we were to get pregnant with more than one fetus, would we elect to abort some of them? Teir and I had a hard time contemplating this question. How could we discuss getting rid of something that we wanted so badly? We decide that our odds would be much higher if we were to have the doctor transfer the maximum number of embryos. We finally decided that if we got pregnant, we would keep them all.

Selective reduction may be a very easy or difficult question for you and your significant other to discuss. I have heard others stat that making the decision to transfer a certain number of embryos conflicted with their desire to parent only one child. Others have stated that they didn't care how many children they had in a single pregnancy. There is no right or wrong answer, but there is a right decision for your life, and it is one that only you and your significant other can make for yourselves.

EGG RETRIEVAL

After I began the medication, I had to go to the endocrinologist office every other day for an ultrasound. The purpose of the ultrasound was for the physician to see my progress with egg production. The physician would look at the number and size of the eggs. In addition, I had to do a blood test to check my FSH (Follicle Stimulating Hormone) Levels. After about two weeks on my medication my physician scheduled me for an egg retrieval appointment. While the egg retrieval was occurring in the office, the procedure was very surgical in nature. I'd go into my operative gown, say goodbye to Teir, and then I was wheeled into the procedure room.

When I was taken into the procedure room Teir had to perform as well. Prior to our appointment he was given specific instructions: no tight pants, no ejaculation within so much time before the appointment, no hot tubs, no marijuana before the appointment, no hot tubs, no marijuana before the appointment, and a lot of other no's. Teir was instructed to go into a room and provide a sample of his semen. The semen was taken to the lab and a semen wash was performed. The quality of the semen was reviewed and held to later be combined with the egg to create an embryo.

Once in the procedure room I was given local anesthetics to sedate me. My physician informed me after the procedure that he used a needle like instrument to vaginally retrieve the eggs. The eggs were sucked into the needle and taken into the lab. Before I left the office, the doctor told me how many eggs were retrieved. Let's just call me fertile mertile, because I would produce so many eggs. It was exciting to discover that I was able to produce so many eggs, but it also brought about some sadness. You see I was sad that my body wanted to do what it had been naturally created to do, produce life. However, it couldn't complete the task of life production. I began to question God. "Why would he give me the ability to produce a large number of quality eggs, but the inability to produce life". I struggled with this feeling throughout the process of IVF and thereafter.

EMBRYO SELECTION

The eggs that were taken from the transfer were fertilized with Teir's Sperm. A few days after the retrieval and fertilization I received a call from the doctor to come into the office to select which eggs we wanted transferred, disposed of and frozen. The doctor informed us that within days after fertilization the embryo's cells would divide, thus the embryo was thriving. At or about five days after fertilization the embryo with the best possibility of making it to a pregnancy is one that makes it to blastocyst. Blastocyst is when the embryo has two distinct cell types and a central cavity filled with fluid. One set of the cells become the placenta and the other the fetus. My doctor showed us the picture of the embryos and gave his advice as to which one was more likely to succeed. The doctor spoke with us about assisted embryo hatching and implantation. Embryo's formulate in a shell called the Zona Pellucida. It is necessary for the embryo to break its shell or hatch so that it can implant to the uterine wall of its mama. Some people may choose to get assistance in the hatching of the shell or Zona Pellucida, due to certain things like age, FSH Levels, or whether the embryo made it to blastocyst.

TRANSFER

We were very lucky that our embryos made it to blastocyst. The cell division looked very promising and the embryo's health and quality was great! The last two very medically descriptive sentences mean my babies growing in a petri dish were looking and doing well. The nurse called me and let me know it was time for us to transfer the embryos we'd selected with our doctor into my womb. She prescribed me Valium to calm me down and scheduled a date.

On the da of my appointment I was a ball of nerves, so the Valium was much appreciated. Teir and I arrived at the infertility center and taken into an exam room. The transfer procedure is quick. The medical staff will ask you to empty part of your bladder. This request is made so that the doctor has a better look at our uterus on the ultrasound machine. While laying on your back he physician will utilize an abdominal ultrasound to look at the location in which to place the embryo. The doctor will use a catheter (pictured on the next page) that contains the embryo's in it to transfer the embryos from the inside of the catheter into the uterine cavity. The process is not the most comfortable due to the fluid remaining in the bladder. In all the times that I have done a transfer, I do not remember any pain associated with the insertion of the catheter into the vagina.

IN VITRO FERTILISATION
Embryo transfer

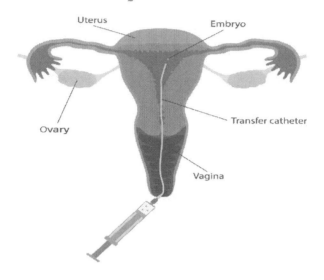

During my transfer, I knew the exact moment the embryos were transferred. I remember at each transfer, the mome the embros were released from the catheter, I saw a small bright light appear on the ultrasound machine screen. In my romanticized thoughts I believed that the small bright light was the beginning of a life in my womb. Within 15 minutes or less the entire transfer process is over. The medical staff asks that you remain lying down a few minutes after the transfer. The moment I stood up I was afraid that the embryo would just slide back out of my womb through my vagina and hit the floor. I walked carefully to the car and took it very easy, although my doctor assured me that it was unnecessary to change my normal activity. The next step was to wait and see if the embryos would implant in my uterus causing me to be pregnant. The doctor could do everything up until this point, but that little part of creating life is still left for God. Unless of course new God like technologies have been created since my experience.

CHAPTER 4

REPEAT, REJECT, REPEAT, REJECT...

THE CYCLE AND COST OF LOSING

THE WAIT

The time after the transfer was the most difficult and exciting time. On the one hand, I was constantly thinking that I was carrying my baby. I walked around carefully thinking that the embryo was trying hard to attached to my uterus. On the other hand, I was worried that the embryo would not attach. A week after the transfer I felt pregnant. My breast felt tender and I was tired. I just knew I was pregnant. Before my appointment to check my pregnancy status, I stopped at Target. I felt a cramping pain and went to the bathroom. Once in the bathroom, I discovered that my period started.

PREGNANCY 3: ECTOPIC

Shortly after our first attempt at IVF Teir and I discovered that we had become pregnant without the assistance of IVF. The end of my first trimester had approached and I was ecstatic hat I had begun to feel pregnant – heavy, tired and bloated. My belly was starting to poke out and I could not be any happier. One morning I woke up and didn't feel well. I felt feverish and crampy. I told Teir that I felt very off that morning. By noon, I asked Teir to call my OB to ask her if my abdominal cramping was the norm. She informed me that many women feel cramping in early pregnancy. She told me to take it easy and contact her again if the cramping got worse, or if I began to bleed more than just mere spotting.

By three in the afternoon, I had begun to spot very lightly. My doctor told me to come to the hospital if it would ease my fears. By four the bleeding had gotten heavier and the cramping more intense. I asked Teir to drive me to Stanford Hospital. The drive to the hospital felt like the longest ride of my life. The pain was so unbearable and seemed to intensify quickly. When we arrived at the hospital I was taken into a room and evaluated. My doctor entered in to the room and she had tears in her eyes. She wiped her eyes and informed me that I had an ectopic pregnancy. She informed me that the baby had grown in my fallopian tube and that the tube ruptured. My doctor finally told me that there was massive bleeding and that they had to rush me into surgery to remove the baby and the tube immediately. Another doctor entered the room and asked if there was anyone that I'd like to call. He told me that they had to rush me into the surgery due to the amount of bleeding I only had 15 minutes to live.

The doctor gave me the phones that they carry on their person around the hospital and told me to call my mom. I called my mom and told her everything and that I loved her very much. Teir and I shared with one another how much we loved one another and then I was rushed to the operating room. After the surgery I learned that my left fallopian tube and baby were removed. The surgeon made a 4-inch bikini cut right underneath my belly button. The weirdest thing was that the hospital had placed me on the maternity ward. My nurse had me get on my feet immediately to start the healing process. I walked around the ward looking at the new parents with their babies being pushed into the room. It was too much for me so close to the loss of my own baby. I asked my nurse if I could be moved to another location and she agreed. I moved to another location in the hospital. I didn't know how to feel and found that I felt a bunch of emotions. I was so sad and depressed. I was motivated to hurry up and get better so that I could return to work and try IVF again. I was encouraged that maybe I could get pregnant on my own again. I was ashamed, because I felt like my body had failed me and now that one of my fallopian tubes was removed, I felt like I was more like a man than a woman.

I was released home and as soon as I got home Teir informed me that he had a work-related trip he had to take to British Columbia. My mom and mother in law came to check on me, bring me food and help me change my bandages. Even though I had people coming to check on me, I felt so alone in the loss of my baby. I deeply appreciated the help from the moms, yet all I wanted was for my husband to return home so we could grieve alone. I didn't feel like women who had given birth could really understand the emotional pain I was experiencing. Weeks after the surgery I felt deeply depressed. I found myself thanking God that he had chosen me to go through infertility and miscarriage rather than my cousins. Other times I pitied myself. I walked around with a smile on my face and told everyone "I'm doing fine"! That statement was so far from the truth. In fact, I felt worthless.

I began to feel incredibly sad for Teir and the fact that due to my issues, maybe he would never be a father. I will never forget going to Teir and telling him that maybe he should leave me and go have a family with another woman. Teir looked at me like I was crazy and told me that I was the only woman that he wanted. I told myself that he didn't mean that and that he probably really did not want to trade in his chance to parent for me. So, I told him that he could go have an affair with "a normal girl" and even get "a normal girl pregnant". I don't think I even contemplated what life would look like for any of us if he took me up on that offer - thank God he didn't! The more time I had off from work to sit and think about what had just happened to me, the deeper into a depressed state I sunk. I decided it was time to seek professional help.

I meet with a young therapist that asked me to tell my story. After hearing my story, which was shortened due to the limited time I had to meet with her, she began to tell me that I was obsessed with babies. She furthered that I shouldn't be a mom until I got help with my weird obsession with just having a baby. I was so upset with her assessment and lack of empathy for my losses. I found a new therapist who really helped me overcome my new issues with my femininity due to the removal of my tube. I really appreciated her suggestion that when I get stuck in a sad thought, that I be mindful and change the channel to a better program.

PREGNANCY 4: TAHOE BABY

When I lost the pregnancy, I felt like I wanted to become pregnant immediately. I didn't trust that my body would do it again on its own. We decided to give IVF another try. IVF was so expensive that we sought out the assistance of our family and friends for help to pay for another fifteen-thousand-dollar cycle. I had my second cycle, yet I still did not get pregnant. I began to wonder if it was going to ever happen for us. People around us began to tell us that we weren't getting pregnant because we were trying too hard. Go figure, the solution to my infertility was to stop trying to get pregnant and to stop thinking about pregnancy when all I could think about was becoming a mom.

Teir and I had become pregnant a few times on our own but each time I lost my pregnancy within the first trimester. Within just a couple of years after attempting to get pregnant through IVF we had gotten pregnant eight times on our own. A few times I thought I was going to make it to the end, but right before my fourth month I would lose the baby. It was so emotionally and physically draining. Sex began to feel more like a task. I felt so desperate that I wanted to try IVF again no matter the cost.

After losing the third pregnancy and having a second failed IVF Attempt, I felt so hopeless and less like a woman. We were running really low on funds and had to decide how we were going to proceed. In our normal fashion we decided to take a short trip to take our minds off the heavy thinking. Teir loves to ski so we decided to go to Lake Tahoe. On the drive to Lake Tahoe I began to feel increasingly sick. Teir had to pull the car over several times so that I could run to the restroom. At each stop I had to vomit as if I had the stomach flu.

When we arrived at the hotel it was so beautiful. The grounds were lit up with white strung holiday lights due to the season. Teir and I were happy to just get away. I noticed that I felt very pregnant and thought maybe we should get a pregnancy test. We checked into the room, went to the pharmacy and then found a place to go have dinner. Near the hotel we found a Chinese Food restaurant. With great anticipation, I excused myself to the restroom to take the pregnancy test. I had no faith that the test would come back positive as none of my test were coming back with a positive result. I peed on the stick and within seconds the test read "pregnant". It was one of the new tests that actually spell out the results. I looked at it again and yes, my test read pregnant. I was in a complete state of shook! I ran from the restroom and showed Teir. I did not care that we were in the middle of a restaurant we had a positive pregnancy test. We were so happy that it was the topic of each conversation we had. With my history we'd decided that it was too risky for me to go skiing. While Teir went skiing, I sat at the lodge and had hot coco and read a book. We were so shocked that we were pregnant without the assistance of IVF. We couldn't believe we got pregnant the "normal" way.

Unfortunately, our excitement came to an end. Within a week after discovering that I was pregnant I began to cramp and discovered that I was miscarrying my baby.

BEGGING THE LADY AT WESTERN CREDIT UNION

Weeks after miscarrying I felt so empty and incomplete. I tried to heal my pain by going shopping. I will never forget the day that I decided to try to heal my pain with shop therapy. I sat in a Nordstrom, grabbed my phone and called Teir. As soon as Teir answered the phone I began crying and pleading with him that I needed at least a thousand dollars to shop with to make me feel better. Teir obliged me and I blew through the thousand dollars in minutes. The expenditure didn't change how sad I had been feeling. I felt even worse that I had blown through money that we desperately needed.

When the shop therapy failed, I began to feel like I needed to leave the condo that we had purchased and start our life in another home. In retrospect, I realize that I used to run from the things that plagues me. So, my first escape was running from reality and trying to spend beyond my means. When that didn't make me feel better, I asked Teir to put the condo we had purchased three years earlier on the market. Instead of putting the condo on the market we decided to rent it out. We found a family to rent it and became landlords. We found our beautiful home in the hills of our hometown Oakland, California. It was exciting, yet I didn't feel like it was helping me move past the pain, depression and anxiety I was facing on a daily basis. I was doing a very great job at concealing how I was truly feeling. So, my next run was to book a two-and-a-half-week international vacation for Teir and I to go on. Teir and I booked a trip to Europe, which included visiting Paris, France; London, England; Rome, Italy, Lucerne, Switzerland, and Florence, Italy. The trip was amazing. I saw things that I had only seen in my history books. However, I still felt locked by my circumstances. I was so locked that I refused to allow myself to fully take in the blessing of all the sites we were seeing and experiences we were having. Sex began to feel like a task and all I could think of was my inability to get pregnant. Then came the fantasy. Maybe I would get pregnant while on vacation and that would be my miracle. It didn't happen.

When we returned home, we discovered that after going on the vacation, purchasing he house and the IVF Cycles, we had depleted our savings. Teir and I went to the bank to get a line of credit to cover our next fertility cycle. My desire to become pregnant was strong. We meet with an African American Woman who resembled one of my aunts. She had us complete our application for the loan. She came back and informed us that we didn't qualify for the full $25k we were seeking. She informed us that she could only approve $10k. I knew $10k was not enough for another cycle. I began to cry so loudly. I dropped to the floor making it to my knees. I wailed out so loud and then began to crawl on my knees to this woman begging for the full amount of money. The woman gently placed her hand under my chin and said, "baby you get up off the floor". I still cried and begged. She told me to get off the floor again. Teir helped me up and we sat down. The woman handed me a tissue, leaned in and said "baby you are too wonderful to ever have to beg for anything. Don't you ever beg man for anything ever again. God is the provider of your needs and he will take care of you". She excused herself so that she could discuss with her boss. When she re-entered, she informed us that she'd gotten authorization to give us $15k.

PREGNANCY 5-8

After I received the funds from the bank, I couldn't wait to get to my doctor to begin another cycle. We went through one more fresh cycle (the type of cycle I have been discussing in this book thus far) and two more frozen cycles (we implanted embryos that we had kept frozen). None of these attempts worked, yet we got pregnant on our own four more times, but none of the pregnancy survived.

TRYING TO COPE WITH SADNESS AND DEPRESSION

I wasn't even thirty and I had gone through so much and lost even more. I had never known such loss and wasn't afforded the tools to cope with all the loss. I had lost eight pregnancies by age 30, been kicked out of law school after getting a B- in a class (my faculty scholarship required B average or higher to remain at the school) and lost my grandfather. I went to see several therapists and even went to see a minister. During the meeting with the minister he gave Teir and I $40 cash and told us to go on a date and a baby would come.

It was as if no one knew what words we needed to hear to help ease the pain we were feeling. I began to read the bible and found a scripture in Galatians 4:27: "Be glad, barren woman, you who never bore a child; shout for joy and cry aloud, you who were never in labor; because more are the children of the desolate woman than of her who has a husband." I had no idea what this scripture meant.

I trusted God and his wonderful plan for my life. Look, God promised me an abundant life and I know he is a God that doesn't lie when it comes to his promises. But what did I have to be glad about? The lack of labor pains, carrying a baby for nine months, gaining weight, swollen ankles, and all the other stuff pregnant women complain about during their pregnancy. I would have given anything to experience any of the above. I tried to smile, think positively, even encourage someone else, but underneath I felt broken. I tried to convince myself and others that despite everything we were going through I was ok with my diagnosis. I constantly thanked God for being the one he chose to have this test. Yet, I learned that when I tried to sweep my infertility under a rug, all I did was place a Band-Aid over a wound that needed stitches.

CHAPTER 5

ENOUGH!!!!

ADOPTION? BUT I WANT MY OWN BABY

After several miscarriages and failed IVF attempts my family and friends began to suggest that I try to become a mom another way. Of course, they were worried about my health. I mean I almost died with the ectopic pregnancy and had been secretly hiding my sadness behind a well-rehearsed smile. Yet, I remember so clearly the moment that I relinquished the hold I placed on myself on my ideology on how I could become a mom. I release the thought that I could only become a parent through the typical biological means. The relinquishment came while visiting Shamu in San Diego.

Teir and I had lost yet another pregnancy and once again we decided to travel. This time we decided we'd go to San Diego. We arrived at our beautiful accommodations and began to plan out what sites we wanted to see. We decided to go to Tijuana Mexico, the Gaslamp District, the House of Blues Sunday Brunch, and SeaWorld. We had been having a great time and working hard to ignore all the pain we had endured with our fertility struggles. We laughed the entire trip. We went to Tijuana and I drove on the wrong side of the street, we watched drunk people karaoke and listen to smooth jazz in the Gaslamp District. But our life changing moment occurred at SeaWorld.

It's very funny how you don't really notice something until you want it. Like a specific car. You desire it and then all of a sudden you see them everywhere you go. An attractive person, when you're in a relationship you don't really pay them attention, but once your single they're everywhere and usually in a relationship with someone else. For me I noticed pregnant women and infants. It seemed like that day at SeaWorld it was the pregnant woman and infant day. They were everywhere and triggering my sadness around my inability to go full term in a pregnancy. Teir and I were standing in line for a ride and began to talk about how sad we both were about not having a baby. As soon as we began to talk, this little Hispanic boy maybe four years of age began to do a bunch of silly things in an attempt to get our attention. He was super cute. A chubby little boy who had enough personality to fill a room. His little belly hung out of his shirt and he slid around trying to make people laugh. Teir turned to me and said, "If we adopt Pana, we can have a cute kid like that little boy". Tears began to roll down my face because until that moment I had never thought I would be ok with mothering a child I had not birthed.

As soon as Teir said "if we adopt Pana, we can have a cute kid like that little boy", I felt like God poured so much into my spirit. In that moment God reminded me of the three figures adopted in the bible. Jesus was adopted by Joseph, Moses by Pharaoh's Daughter Hatshepsut, and Ester by her cousin. A rush of thoughts overcame me in that very moment. I thought if God called these people to adopt Moses, Jesus and Ester, then maybe he was calling me to become an adoptive mom. My next thought was, "How dare you deny God's calling"? As Teir and I watched Shamu the Whale perform, all I could think about was adoption and the possibility that maybe I would be a mom, through that vessel.

SeaWorld was eye opening, but I still struggled with my desire to birth a child. Did adoption mean I was giving up on trying to get pregnant? I sat around thinking about our babies' physical features and other attributes. I began to look into adoption agencies, but there was no urgency in my search. I began to forget what God had whispered into my spirit at SeaWorld and began to wallow in self-pity and unworthiness. Shortly after returning home from SeaWorld, I as watching a reality TV show that was out at the time called Run's House. The show feature Reverend Run of the famous hip hop group Run DMC, his wife Justine and their blended family. On the show Justine and Run suffered the loss of their baby. Justine gave birth to a baby girl Victoria, who died shortly after being born. What Justine and Run displayed for the world in their moment of loss was amazing and inspiring. In their grief, they displayed strength, love, faith, and integrity. Shortly after their loss they adopted a daughter Miley. A few weeks after the show aired, I was so touched and inspired to continue on my adoption journey. My adoption search began!

ADOPTION AGENCIES

Teir and I had no clue where to start our adoption search. We began our search on the internet. We learned that we had so many options and choices when it came to adoption. There are independent and agency adoptions; foster adoption, international and domestic adoptions. After completing my online research, I found myself to be even more confused than before I had begun.

I talked to Teir to weigh out our options. One thing we decided was to continue with trying to become pregnant on our own, while going through the process of adoption. I was still in great grief and sadness behind the countless number of pregnancies I had already lost. The more I researched I began to feel closer to becoming a mom. It felt so empowering to purchased books from Barnes and Noble titled the The Whole Life Adoption Book by Jayne Schooler and Thomas Atwood and The Complete Adoption Book, by Laura Beauvais and Raymond Godwin. As I read the chapters of these books, I felt as if it was bringing me one step closer to my child. My mind began to wonder; would I adopt a boy or a girl, what my child would look like, or would we be the same race?

At first Teir and I pondered the thought of adoption from the county agency that conducted foster adoptions. We went to an informational meeting and learned that there was a great need for adoptive and foster parents in our local county. We went to an informational meeting and learned that there was a great need for adoptive and foster parents in our local county. We also learned that the county tries reunification, that is trying to reunify the parent to the child, prior to placement for adoption. We also learned that we could not be very selective about our "match". While we really wanted to be parents, we were very honest about our desires not to become first time parents to a child who had been exposed to drugs in the uterus. We also wanted to parent a newborn and not an older child. It was based on the foregoing reasons that we chose not to adopt through the foster care system.

I began to research international adoptions. There was so much to learn. The first was which country to choose from: Honduras, China, or Ethiopia. Next, what was the cost and the timeline. There was so much to learn, and I knew there was no way we'd be able to make the decision without the assistance of an expert. In my researching I learned of a local adoption agency called Heartsent Adoptions. The staff at Heartsent gave us a warm welcome and the director Val Free had the biggest heart, expertise and wisdom. After our informational, Teir and I began to research domestic adoptions as well. We learned that there were African American Children that could be adopted fairly quickly. We contemplated all our options and decided to adopt domestically.

The adoption process had many steps that involved a number of professionals. We hired Heartsent to complete the home study. We were referred to Attorney David Baum located in Encino, California, to complete the adoption. Teir and I flew immediately to meet Mr. Baum in Encino. Mr. Baum was a delightful man. When he spoke, you felt like you had just met the man who does the movie phone voice. While David was a businessman, he had a big heart. As our conversation with David progressed, I came to learn why he had a big heart. David informed us that he and his wife were adoptive parents. Teir and I learned of the entire adoption process which began with working with an agency to get the adoption screening, called a home study completed, drafting our dear birthmother letter and then wait on our match. We learned that the agency fee with Heartsent was going to be approximately $6,000 and the cost with David Baum was $15,000. We also learned that there would be additional cost to work with another firm, Adams Romer (Currently Adams, Romer, Stoeckenius, and Wotherspoon LLP), as they would work with the birth mother and work with Mr. Baum to complete the post placement agreements. The Cost with Adams and Romer was approximately $8000. The cost of adopting for us was about $30,000. What helped with the cost was the service providers willingness to allow us to make payments. Here are a few things to ask and consider when interviewing a service provider in your adoption:

1. Years of experience - This didn't matter to me as much as how often the provider was actually placing and matching families.

2. How they located birthmothers - I wanted to know how birthmother are selected and what type of screening was had on the birthmothers. For example, we interviewed with a birthmother that used Crystal Meth her entire pregnancy. We weren't sure we would be ok with this match. It became clear that it's very important to let your service provider know what you will and will not accept. Do this unapologetically, you don't have to accept things that you are not comfortable with. Your match is out there!

3. Number of adoptions per year - This was so important to me! Did I want to go with a service provider that had one match per year or 100? of course the more matches the higher my chances of a match in a lower amount of wait time.

4. Cost - Adoptions may range from $10k to $45K depending on the type of adoption.

5. Does the cost vary if the child is of a particular ethnicity, has been exposed to drugs, or has a disability or developmental delay?

6. What other providers you will need in the process and the cost of additional services - This is huge! Ask about the cost of social workers, reports, fingerprinting, cost associated with adopting from another state, post adoption cost, birthmother cost, and more. Get the full picture on the rate!

7. If they have a payment schedule.

8. Scholarships?

9. If you will get guidance with the dear birth parent/mother letter.

10. What is a realistic timeline?

THE ADOPTION PROCESS

Once we paid our deposit the journey began. Heartsent Adoptions gave me lots of paperwork to complete to begin the home study. The home study involved us providing information about our financial and medical status. We also had to meet with a social worker/therapist on several occasions in our home and her office. While she was investigating us, she never made us feel interrogated or less than. I learned in the process that it was important to remain authentic. I read where people would over clean their home or try to bake cookies so that the aroma would be in the air when their worker arrived for the home visit. It's not necessary to be anything other than yourself in this process. Your child will come to know you, not a made-up version of yourself. So, it's imperative that you and your partner remain true to yourself to get to the child God intended for you to parent.

Completing the home study paperwork was exhausting, but it made me feel as if I was moving closer to becoming a mom. Teir and I decided that at this point we would only share that we were adopting with a few people. Our next step was to write a dear birthmother letter. The letter would be the first contact potential birth mothers had with us. Instead of it being a stressful thing, Teir and I had a lot of fun creating our dear birth mother letter. We found great pictures of us and our family members. We talked about our love for each other and our families, our hobbies, our careers and our desires to become parents. The final product was great, and we were so ready to get it out (a copy of one of our letters is at the end of this book). The next step was the wait!

We began to receive calls about potential matches. The beauty in adoption is that matching is not a one-way street. It has to be a mutual decision by the birth parent(s) and the adoptive parent(s). We began to speak with birth mothers on the phone first. If the conversation progressed than we would schedule a meeting in person. We spoke with a 14-year-old mother to be and her aunt. She and the birth father had made the decision to place their baby for adoption. Teir and I went to Los Angeles to meet her and attend one of her prenatal appointments. After spending time with one another, we made the decision to adopt her baby.

Once we made the connection, the paperwork to adopt her baby began. We continued to be in contact with she and her aunt. As her due date approached, I learned that I was pregnant, but the pregnancy resulted in a miscarriage. Shortly after the miscarriage I received a phone call stating that the young mother and her aunt had changed their mind. It was devastating to lose my pregnancy and the adoptive child I had mentally began to connect with. We took a little time to recover, thanked god that she was able to parent and that he was holding us out for the child who was created just for Teir and I.

Note: Gratitude even when it feels like a loss is what will keep you sane in this process. It is imperative to trust the process and know that there is a child meant just for you and your partner.

SWEET JUSTICE

Within months we received a call that there was a baby boy in Chicago due to be born in June 2009. We spoke with the birth mother and fell in love! After several conversations on the phone with her, we collectively decided that we were a match. I will expand with more details of our experience in my next book "The Good, the Bad and Ugly of Adoptions". We flew to Chicago and witnessed the birth of our first child Justice. As we left the hospital, I could not believe I was really a mom. Due to interstate requirements, we had to stay in Chicago until we received permission to take a resident of the State of Illinois to the State of California to be adopted. The time in Illinois with just the three of us was precious and beautiful. That time alone allowed us to spend time without the distractions of people coming to see the new baby. We spent the majority of our time in the hotel room bonding with the baby. Once we were permitted to leave, we returned home and began our lives together, with our sweet little baby boy Justice.

MY BABY BOY AIDEN

Parenting Justice was a joy, he's such an amazing boy! The adoption process wasn't too bad. When Justice was three years old, Teir and I decided we wanted to experience the joy of becoming a parent again. Teir came to me and said Justice would be better off if he had a sibling. The search began for our next child. We had to modify the dear birthmother letter because now we needed to let potential matches know that we had a child. In 2012 we began the process again and it led us to our second son Aiden.

We received a phone call from the lawyers at Adams, Romer, Stoeckenius, and Wotherspoon, LLP about a potential match. We learned that a woman had been in a very abusive situation with the biological father of her unborn child and that she was due to deliver the next morning. Teir and I spoke with her that night and decided that it was a great fit. However, we weren't ready to bring a baby home the next day. The fact that the child that was coming was a boy made the decision easier as we had a bunch of clothing for a baby boy. We pulled Justice's baby items out and prepared for the baby that same night. We meet the birth mother and her current boyfriend (not the baby's father) at the hospital. She and I went into labor and delivery for her C-Section. When Aiden, arrived he was 5 pounds and needed to go directly to the neonatal intensive care unit (NICU).

The doctors told me I could go with Aiden, but I couldn't leave his birth mother all alone. Once in the NICU, things got crazy! Aiden's biological father appeared at the hospital and threatened to blow up the hospital if he couldn't take the baby. It was very scary for the biological mother, who was seeking a restraining order for his prior acts of violence towards her, and us. Aiden remained in the hospital for three weeks. During the first two weeks I spent the majority of my time going to feed Aiden every two hours and going to court on the restraining order against bio dad and for the adoption. At the conclusion of the two weeks and on my birthday, I received a call not to return to the hospital because the biological mom decided not to place him for adoption. I also received a call that same day that she was at the bank cashing a check for her hotel accommodations, after birth clothing and money for other things allowed and necessary for birth mothers placing their babies.

Losing Aiden hurt bad because Teir and I had really begun to bond with him. Approximately a week later we received a call to go bond with him. Approximately a week later we received a call to go get Aiden from the hospital or the hospital was going to call social services which could result in him being placed in foster care. We took Aiden home and heavy litigation for his adoption ensued. During the litigation process we learned that Aiden had a rare chromosomal disorder that may cause him to never walk or speak. We had several doctors' appointments, court hearings, and medical professionals in our home on a daily basis. Life and marriage became stressful. The sweetest thing was the two children we had been blessed with.

Eventually, we won the case in the adoption of Aiden. Once the dust seemed to settle, we learned that Aiden had a bleeding disorder and that he was Autistic. Despite all these medical issues Aiden is such a wonderful child. He can walk, speak, and he is extremely intelligent. He has developmental delays, but we couldn't imagine our life without him.

THE JOURNEY FROM INFERTILITY TO ADOPTION

Teir and I told countless counselors that the issues we had with infertility and adoption made us stronger as a couple. I actually remember sitting in a counseling session with him and remember us agreeing that we thrived as a couple in the face of adversity. What we thrived at was wearing a smile when we both felt like crying. In our attempt to cope with so much loss and let down we failed to take care of our marriage and grew apart. We eventually dealt with our depression in our own destructive manner, until we realized that we were better to ourselves and the boys divorced. We divorced, sold the family residence and purchased two homes right near each other so that we could co-parent the boys effectively. Justice and Aiden are thriving and so are we!

At the beginning of my journey to motherhood I was hopeful and optimistic. As I walked down the aisle to get married, I wrote the story of my life. I saw the type of house I would live in, the type of job I'd have, the amount of money I would make, and the number of children I would have. However, 365 days after I got married, my life didn't look anything like the story I wrote on my wedding day. This was because things did not go according to MY PLANS. I didn't get pregnant easily, and when I did get pregnant, I began to tell myself that my body was a failure. I began to believe the thoughts that I put in my head and what others told me, that this was somehow all my fault. Maybe I had done something wrong, maybe it was the abortion, and that's why this was happening to me!

Lies, lies, lies... all I did was kept telling myself lies. The truth of the matter is that I was so obsessed with believing that I could not get pregnant or carry a baby the normal way, that I couldn't even see that there were other ways for me to become a mom. Isn't it funny that sometimes when we obsess over living life according to how we've planned it, we miss out on the beauty of God's divine plan for our lives? Not only could I not see the other ways that I could become a parent, I also wasn't allowing myself to see the positive things that was occurring in my live. I was choosing to live in my sad story and not in all the joy I was living and co-creating. During the years of struggling with my infertility, I taught hundreds of high school teenagers who have since thanked me for believing and supporting their goals, I opened a bridal store in the middle of a mall and used the proceeds from my sales for charitable purposes, I obtained my Juris Doctorate and passed the State of California Bar Exam on the first try, I purchased three homes with one being built from the ground up, I opened three law firms, helped my church win souls, raised over $100k for non-profits, had a marriage of 15 years, found love after loss, was a good mom and daughter, and adopted two amazing sons! My cup was running over, and I was operating as if it was empty.

After much needed prayer and therapy, I learned it was time to rewrite my story. It was time to change my perspective, shift my paradigm, or as one therapist told me "Pa'tanisha, it's time to change the channel, this program is worn out". On the heels of great advice, I made the shift and committed to the change. This time I was going to write the story of my life based on reality and with God's direction. First, I had to accept that I did nothing to cause my infertility. Second, I had resolved that I was not broken and what was happening to me did not define me. Finally, I began to realize that I am more than enough, a woman that is fearfully and wonderfully made! This sounds so easy to do, but I suggest seeking the assistance of others to support you in making your shift and re-writing your story.

Now that I refuse to allow what happened to me to define me, I operate in gratitude rather than depression and sorrow. Don't get me wrong, going through infertility and miscarrying eleven pregnancies is a traumatic and horrible series of events to happen to anyone. Yet, I don't have to live the rest of my life a victim of my circumstances. By changing the narrative, I changed the outcome. I am now living my best life! Delay did not equal denial and I work every day to be the best me and the best mom I can be!

DEAR BIRTH MOTHER LETTER
(Personal Photos Have Been Removed)

Dear New Friend,

As a family, we would like to thank you for your consideration and for taking the time to get to know more about us. We cannot begin to know how difficult the journey that brought you to us has been. However, we do know that there is no mistake in your reading this letter. You must be considering adoption out of the greatest love for your child. It is for that reason that we believe you to be a selfless and caring person. While you are making one of the biggest decisions for your life, we hope that we can make it less difficult by providing you with information about us. It is our hope that what you discover from our letter is that we are a very loving family that desires a new member to share our love with.

About Us

We really hold one another in high regard. What Patanisha admires most about Téir is his compassionate and beautiful spirit. She loves seeing the father that he is to their son. He is a wonderful husband, father and best friend. In his presence Patanisha feels safe and protected. He is a very patient, tolerant and loving parent. Our son has his father wrapped very tightly around his finger. Téir always calls Patanisha his superwoman because she can literally do it all. His family often teases that she is the Black Martha Stewart, because she will fix things around the house, take care of Justice's every need, host an awesome party, and cook a meal all the same day. She is often described as thoughtful, giving, energetic, and caring. She and Justice have a really special bond. Both Téir and Patanisha believe in the power of God and love helping others.

Many people don't believe it, but we are true high school sweethearts. We met during the summer of 1993, when a mutual friend introduced us. Initially, we decided to become best friends. A year later and after many conversations a budding love for one another began. Throughout high school and most of college, we dated. Life took us in two different directions that caused us to part ways in 2000. Two years later, we reconnected and picked up right where we left off. During the summer of 2003 we were married. As a couple we both had a strong desire to have a big family, however over the years we struggled with infertility. Although our struggle with infertility was tough, we feel really blessed because what we didn't know was that it would lead us to our son Justice, aka "JJ".

In the early months of 2009, we were matched with a wonderful birth mother. In just a few weeks we fell in love with her and knew there was no mistake that she was the mother of our child. In June of 2009 our baby boy Justice was born right before our eyes. Raising Justice has been more than a joy for us. He is a very sweet, goofy, intelligent, and kind hearted. Justice is very gentle and can't wait to have a sibling. He loves exotic animals and is the only two-year-old that we know that can identify and name a buffalo, a walrus, a lemur, and tell the difference between different wild felines.

We love to travel. Teir and I traveled to Italy (Rome and Florence), Switzerland (Lucerne), France (Paris), London, St. Tomas and the Caribbean. Of all the places we have traveled, Paris is our favorite. Upon arriving in Paris, our tour bus took us to the Eiffel Tower. As soon as we saw the tower it lit up to the most beautiful sight we had ever seen. Who would have thought that a huge piece of metal could stir up so much emotion in two people? We felt so blessed to see new parts of the world and found ourselves saying, "I can't wait to bring our kids here one day". Since his birth Justice has been to Washington, D.C., Chicago, Nevada to see the snow, and in celebration of our nine years of marriage we took him to Disneyland to see all his favorite characters. As soon as he gets a little larger, we plan to take him to places around the world.

A good and solid education is important to us. Each of us attended Historical black Colleges in the south. Of or separate degrees, Patanisha received a Bachelor of Arts in Psychology, a Master of Arts in Change Leadership, and a Juris Doctorate in Law. Téir received a Bachelor of Arts in Business and has a Master of Arts in Public Administration. Patanisha is currently an attorney. She does a lot of pro bono legal work to people who are unable to afford representation. She also owns a bridal store in their local mall. Prior to becoming a lawyer, Patanisha was a high school teacher. Téir works as an accountant. He loves numbers and manages the city's police and firemen retirement plan. Téir is also works as a referee to little league football and basketball. He loves refereeing, but with such little guys, aged 6-13, he often finds that he often has to dry some little guys tears, give support, and encouragement to the young men. While Téir and Patanisha are very ambitious, they always put family first. When Justice was born, Patanisha took of from work for the first two years. Teir and

Patanisha often take Justice on weekend getaways and are both at home every night to eat, bathe, pray with, and tuck in their son. Justice has gotten the work ethic too because he told his parents that he wants a job too! When asked what kind he said, "playing and watching Scooby Doo".

Both of us were raised in Northern California and absolutely love our hometown. Growing up we both dreamed of one day living in a nice home located in an upper middle-class neighborhood. Six years ago, we did just that and purchased our home in the East Bay Hills. The house has three bedrooms and two and a half baths. Visitors often describe our house as relaxing and serene. Justices room is jungle themed and we hope to transform the room connected to his into another babies' room. We all love our backyard, because it is wonderful for family functions. The yard is lovely and Japanese inspired, with a large deck for barbeques, a hot tub and even an outdoor shower. Since Patanisha loves the smell of Jasmine we planted lots of it in the backyard. The front yard is just as beautiful and Téir keeps it well groomed. We have wonderful neighbors and a block filled with many children. There is a great school and two parks within walking distance. Justice just began attending a preschool right down the street from our house which he loves.

Family ties are extremely important to us. Both of us are blessed to have a large, loving, and supportive family. Between the two of us we have four siblings. However, Patanisha is one of thirty-four grandchildren raised as brothers and sisters. Our families all reside in northern California, with the exception of distant relatives in Atlanta, Louisiana, Canada, and Puerto Rico. Our families have been so loving and spoils our son. They have been telling us they are ready for our family to grow again. All of us enjoy skiing, traveling, playing team sports like softball or volleyball, and meeting for Sunday Dinner. With such a large family it is quite a sight to see so many people gathered for dinner.

There are many beliefs we want to pass onto our children. Both of us believe in living spiritually with a belief in God, loving unconditionally, thinking positively, looking beyond the faults of others, and that honesty and integrity are of the most important traits to embody. We want our children to know that they can do anything they set their minds to do and to be. Just as we do for each other, we plan to tell our children that we love them as much as possible. We know that we spoil our child, but we plan to teach our children that it takes hard work to achieve one's greatest potential. The three of us are eager to welcome another member to our family to shower with love, happiness, and the fullness that life has to offer.

Warmest Regards,

Teir, Patanisha, and Justice

Made in the USA
Columbia, SC
14 September 2019